MEET NAOMI OSAKA

PERCY LEED

Lerner Publications ◆ Minneapolis

Lerner Publications Company
An imprint of Lerner Publishing Group, Inc.
241 First Avenue North
Minneapolis, MN 55401 USA

For reading levels and more information, look up this title at www.lernerbooks.com.

Main body text set in Aptifer Slab LT Pro. Typeface provided by Linotype AG.

Editor: Annie Zheng

Library of Congress Cataloging-in-Publication Data

Names: Leed, Percy, 1968– author.
Title: Meet Naomi Osaka : tennis superstar / Percy Leed.
Description: Minneapolis, MN : Lerner Publications, [2025] | Series: Sports VIPs (Lerner sports) | Includes bibliographical references and index. | Audience: Ages 7–11 | Audience: Grades 4–6 | Summary: "Tennis player Naomi Osaka is a four-time Grand Slam singles champion. She competed at her first WTA final in 2016 when she was just eighteen. Readers explore her life and career"— Provided by publisher.
Identifiers: LCCN 2024022874 (print) | LCCN 2024022875 (ebook) | ISBN 9798765649275 (library binding) | ISBN 9798765662472 (paperback) | ISBN 9798765658598 (epub)
Subjects: LCSH: Osaka, Naomi, 1997-—Juvenile literature. | Women tennis players—Japan—Biography—Juvenile literature. | Women tennis players—United States—Biography—Juvenile literature. | Women Olympic athletes—Japan—Biography—Juvenile literature.
Classification: LCC GV994.O73 L44 2025 (print) | LCC GV994.O73 (ebook) | DDC 796.342092 [B]—dc23/eng/20240520

LC record available at https://lccn.loc.gov/2024022874
LC ebook record available at https://lccn.loc.gov/2024022875

Manufactured in the United States of America
1-1011067-53539-8/21/2024

TABLE OF CONTENTS

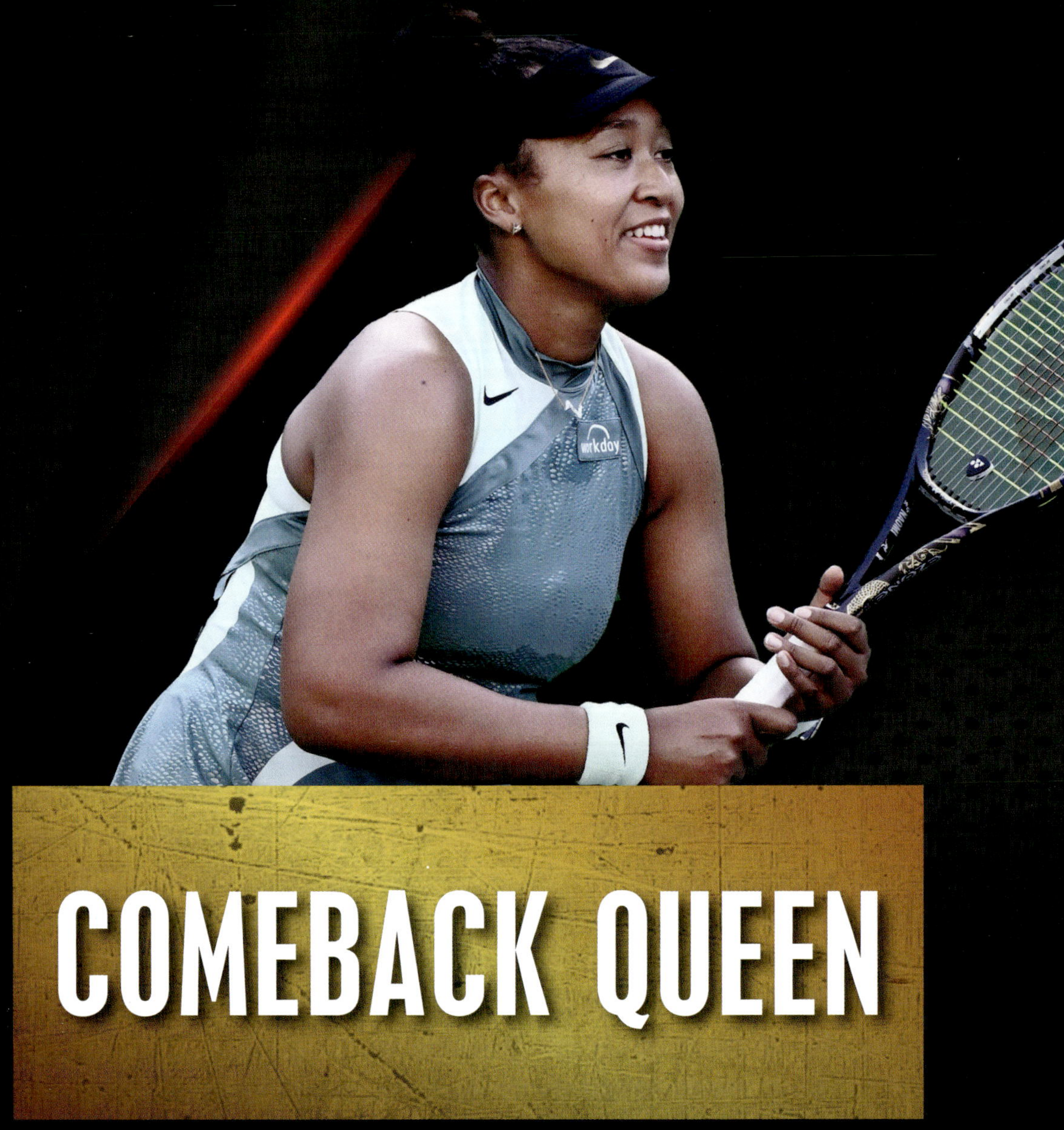

COMEBACK QUEEN

Whack! Naomi Osaka's tennis racket smacked the ball and sent it zooming over the net. Her opponent, Ukraine's Elina Svitolina, was ready for the serve. She sent the ball back.

The two rallied the ball. It sailed from one corner of the court to the other. Svitolina then made a mistake. Her foot slipped. She hit the ball too soft and high. Osaka smacked the ball down on Svitolina's side of the court, winning the point.

FAST FACTS

DATE OF BIRTH: October 16, 1997
POSITION: singles tennis player
LEAGUE: Women's Tennis Association (WTA)

PROFESSIONAL HIGHLIGHTS: became a pro tennis player at the age of 15; won the US Open in 2018 and 2020; won the Australian Open in 2019 and 2021

PERSONAL HIGHLIGHTS: was born in Osaka, Japan; began playing tennis at the age of three; had her first child in July 2023

Osaka and Svitolina were playing at the Miami Open in March 2024. The tournament in Miami, Florida, is a WTA event. Svitolina was the world's 17th-ranked player. Osaka was ranked 229.

Osaka had won the first set 6–2. But the second set was tougher. She and Svitolina traded games back and forth. Neither wanted to lose the lead.

Osaka served the ball. Svitolina struck it back. But it was no contest. Within a few hits, Osaka got the better of Svitolina.

Osaka hit the ball deep into the corner. Svitolina raced to hit it back. It bounced and went out of bounds. Osaka won!

The returning tennis superstar had taken a break for all of 2023. But Osaka looked right at home on the court just a few months into the 2024 WTA season. "I definitely do think it was one of my best matches, if not the best match," she said of her match with Svitolina. "But I also want myself to play better and better every match."

Fans cheer on Osaka as she wins her match against Svitolina.

CHAPTER 1

A FAMILY PLAN

Leonard Francois grew up in Haiti and attended college in New York. Around 1990, he went to study in Japan. That's where he met Tamaki Osaka and fell in love. In April 1996, the couple had their first daughter, Mari. Then, 18 months later, on October 16, 1997, Naomi was born in Osaka, Japan.

In 1999, Francois watched on TV as Venus and Serena Williams played tennis at the French Open. Their story was famous. Their father had never played pro tennis. But starting when his daughters were young, he pushed and trained them to play. By 1999, they were two of the best players in the world.

Venus (*left*) and Serena Williams (*right*) are considered two of the best tennis players of all time. They led the WTA in singles and doubles for years.

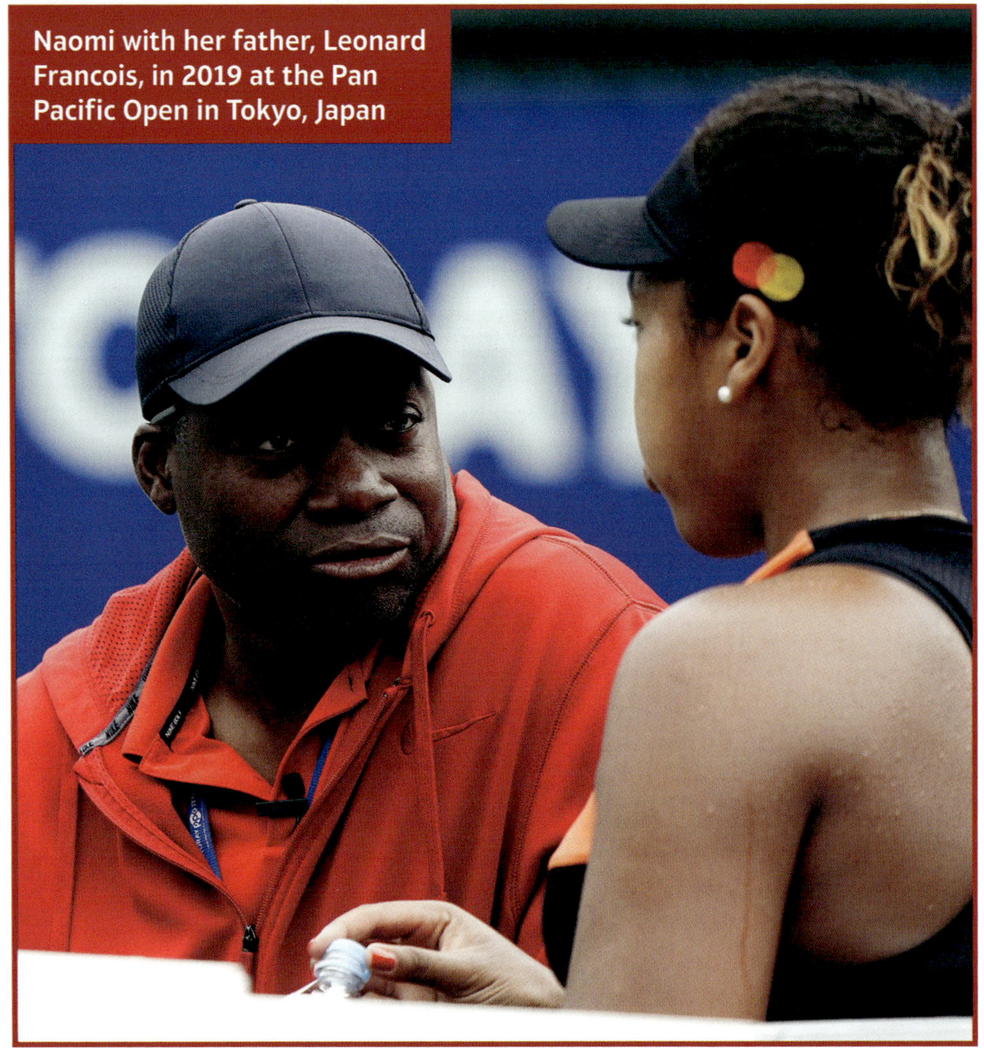

The success of the Williams family inspired Francois. He wanted Naomi and Mari to become as successful as Venus and Serena Williams. As part of his plan, Francois moved the family to New York when Naomi was three. Right away, Francois started tennis lessons with the girls.

Naomi and Mari trained together on public tennis courts. As they grew stronger, Francois pushed them harder. Each sister took thousands of practice swings a day. The sisters also played against each other.

But the 18-month age difference was too much for Naomi to overcome. She always lost, often without winning a single set. "Every day I'd say, 'I'm going to beat you tomorrow,'" Naomi said. Trying to win against her sister helped Naomi get better. It would take 12 years before she could defeat Mari.

In 2006, Francois decided to focus on tennis full-time. The family moved again, this time to Pembroke Pines, Florida. Florida's warm weather allowed Naomi and Mari to play outside all year. Their parents began to homeschool them so they would have even more time for tennis.

The family's focus on tennis paid off. In 2013, Naomi became a pro player at the age of 15.

Osaka playing as pro player in the 2014 Bank of the West Classic in Stanford, California

CHAPTER 2

CLIMBING THE RANKINGS

Osaka played her first pro games soon after. She played at the Challenge Bell in Quebec City, Canada, and the Pan Pacific Open in Tokyo, Japan. She didn't make it past

In 2014, she beat the world's 19th-ranked player Samantha Stosur. It was a major upset since Osaka was still only ranked 406. Osaka played four rounds at the Bank of the West Classic. Before the end of the season, she broke into the top 300 rankings.

Osaka kept climbing the rankings in 2015. Thanks to being ranked high enough, she was able to play at two Grand Slam tournaments. She finished the year strong at rank 144.

Osaka serves the ball against Dominika Cibulkova at the 2016 Pan Pacific Open.

Her best performance so far came in 2016 at the Pan Pacific Open in Tokyo. She beat the 12th-ranked player Dominika Cibulkova in an upset. When asked about how she felt winning against Cibulkova, Osaka said, "I never really care too much about people's rankings. . . . I went out there with a plan and I'm really happy that it worked."

Osaka sprints to return the ball in her match against Svitolina.

Osaka didn't stop there. She fought a hard battle in the semifinals against the 19th-ranked player Elina Svitolina. Osaka won and made it to her first WTA final at the age of 18.

She didn't win the final, but it was the farthest Osaka had ever made it in a WTA tournament. She also entered the top 50 in WTA rankings for the first time. The WTA named Osaka Newcomer of the Year.

In 2017, Osaka pulled off upsets against many top-ranked players, including Anastasija Sevastova, Angelique Kerber, and Venus Williams. Two of them were top-10 players. Soon, Osaka would reach the top ranks herself.

In 2017, Osaka won against tennis star Venus Williams, who was ranked number five at the time.

CHAPTER 3

OPEN FOR BUSINESS

Osaka's WTA breakthrough came at the 2018 US Open. She entered the tournament as the 20th-ranked player. But no one could keep up with her strength and power. She faced Serena Williams in the final match and won both sets.

Winning the US Open skyrocketed Osaka's popularity around the world. Companies took notice. Her image appeared on products such as instant noodles. She signed deals to endorse products for Nike, Mastercard, and others. In 2019, *Forbes* magazine said Osaka was the second-highest-paid female athlete in the world.

Nissin Foods, most well known for their instant noodles, signed a deal with Osaka in 2016 for her to endorse their products.

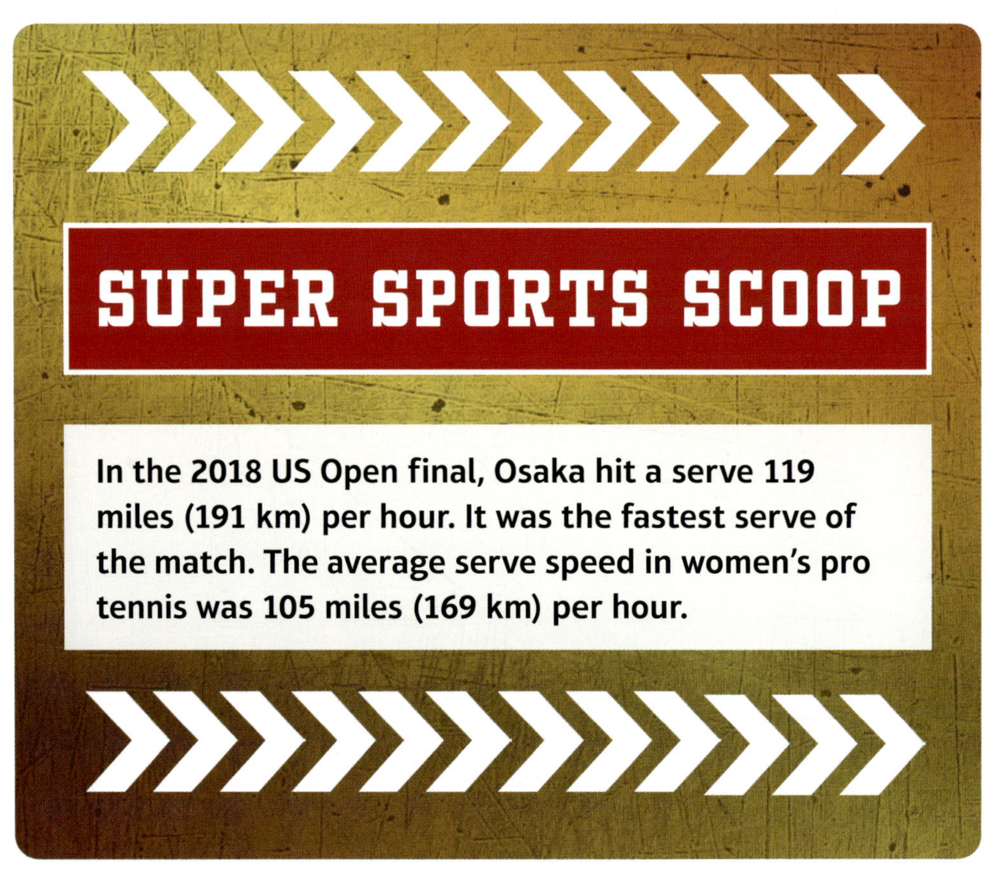

About five months after winning the US Open, Osaka entered the 2019 Australian Open. Fans expected her to do well. She didn't disappoint them. Osaka reached the championship match against the eighth-ranked player Petra Kvitova. Both players fought hard for the title. Osaka won after playing three tough sets. She was the 2019 Australian Open champion!

After she won in Australia, the WTA ranked Osaka the world's top female tennis player. She is the first person from Asia to rank at the top of the men's or women's rankings. She stayed number one for six months.

In September 2019, Osaka won the Pan Pacific Open in Osaka, Japan, the city where she was born. The next month she won the China Open. It was her second victory in a row.

At the 2020 US Open in September, Osaka made it to the final. She faced Victoria Azarenka, the 27th-ranked player in the world. Osaka beat Azarenka in three sets to win the tournament for the second time. She took time off after this tournament to heal from a leg injury.

Osaka winning her second US Open in 2020

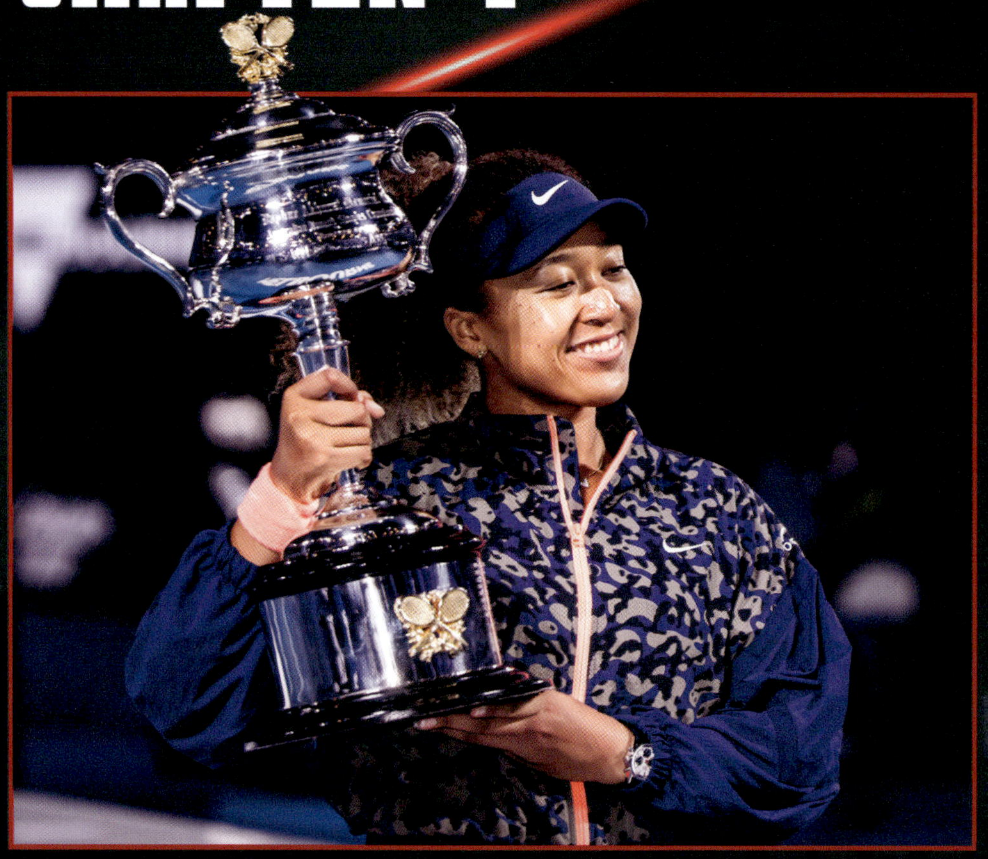

CHAPTER 4

STAR PLAYER

At the start of the 2021 WTA tour, Osaka came back to the court in full swing. She entered the Australian Open and crushed her opponents. Osaka swept the final, becoming the Australian Open champion once more. It was her fourth Grand Slam title.

But not everything went smoothly for Osaka. In May 2021, Osaka said that she would not talk to the press for the French Open. All players must talk to reporters. Not doing it means players can be fined or removed from the tournament. But Osaka chose to take the $15,000 fine.

Osaka played one round at the 2021 French Open before withdrawing from the tournament.

"I've often felt that people have no regard for athletes' mental health, and this rings very true whenever I see a press conference or partake in one," Osaka wrote on social media. Reporters often ask athletes the same questions again and again. They might ask about things athletes don't wish to discuss. This can harm an athlete's mental health.

Osaka is a strong advocate for mental health. She hoped that the money she paid for the fine would go

toward a mental health charity. She later dropped out of the French Open to take care of her own mental health.

Osaka had been battling depression for years. Tennis didn't bring her the enjoyment it used to. When she won, she said it felt more like relief than happiness. She took another break from tennis after the US Open in September.

With the support of her friends and family, Osaka came back to tennis in 2022. Her main goal this time was to have fun.

She didn't make it very far in the 2022 Australian Open. She only made it to the third round. Her loss meant that her rank would drop down into the 70s for the first time in four years. But she said she was happy despite the loss.

Osaka later took another break in 2023. This time, she stepped away to become a mother. Osaka and rapper Cordae welcomed their child, Shai, in July 2023.

The 2024 Brisbane International in January marked Osaka's next return to pro tennis. She was ranked in the 800s. After that, she played in more tournaments. She won three rounds at the Italian Open. This shot her rank up to 134.

Osaka's tennis journey has been a roller coaster. Mental health breaks and a baby had her briefly step away from the court. But nothing could keep her away from her love of the sport. "It was so fun to play in an atmosphere like this again," she said of playing WTA events in 2024. "I'm excited to see how far I can go and where life takes me."

NAOMI OSAKA CAREER STATS

HIGHEST RANKING:
1

GRAND SLAM TITLES:
4

SINGLES TITLES:
7

PRIZE MONEY:
$21,797,363

SINGLES WINS:
282

Stats are accurate through August 14, 2024.

GLOSSARY

advocate: someone who publicly supports a cause

endorse: recommend a product or service, usually in exchange for money

fine: money that is owed as punishment for an action

Grand Slam: one of the four major WTA championships

homeschool: to teach school subjects to one's children at home

press: members of the media such as reporters

rally: a series of shots between players before a point is won

serve: to hit the ball to begin play

set: a group of six or more games

singles: a tennis match with one player on each side

upset: when someone beats the player or team that was expected to win

Women's Tennis Association (WTA): the governing body of women's pro tennis

SOURCE NOTES

7   2024 Miami, "The Osaka Comeback Journey Continues with Statement Win against Svitolina," WTA Tour, March 23, 2024, https://www.wtatennis.com/news/3940170/the-osaka -comeback-journey-continues-with-statement-win-against -svitolina.

11   Brook Larmer, "Naomi Osaka's Breakthrough Game," *New York Times*, August 23, 2018, https://www.nytimes.com/2018/08/23 /magazine/naomi-osakas-breakthrough-game.html.

15   Andrew McKirdy, "Overpowering Osaka Eliminates Cibulkova," *Japan Times*, September 21, 2016, https://www .japantimes.co.jp/sports/2016/09/21/tennis/overpowering -osaka-eliminates-cibulkova/.

24   Jill Martin, "Naomi Osaka Says She Won't Do Press Conferences during the French Open," CNN, May 27, 2021, https://www.cnn.com/2021/05/26/tennis/naomi-osaka-no -press-conferences-at-french-open-spt-intl/index.html.

27   Baseline staff, "After Miami Open Effort, Naomi Osaka Says She's 'Excited to See How Far I Can Go,'" *Tennis*, March 29, 2024, https://www.tennis.com/baseline/articles/after-miami -open-effort-naomi-osaka-says-she-s-excited-to-see-how-far -i-can-go.

LEARN MORE

Britannica Kids: Naomi Osaka

https://kids.britannica.com/kids/article/Naomi-Osaka/634244

Doeden, Matt. *Trailblazing Women in Tennis*. Chicago: Norwood House, 2023.

Fishman, Jon M. *Tennis's G.O.A.T.: Serena Williams, Roger Federer, and More*. Minneapolis: Lerner Publications, 2022.

Golkar, Golriz. *Naomi Osaka*. Minneapolis: Bellwether Media, 2024.

Kiddle: Naomi Osaka Facts for Kids

https://kids.kiddle.co/Naomi_Osaka

Kiddle: Women's Tennis Association Facts for Kids

https://kids.kiddle.co/Women%27s_Tennis_Association

INDEX

PHOTO ACKNOWLEDGMENTS

Image credits: AP Photo/John Cordes/Icon Sportswire, p. 4; AP Photo/hoo-me.com/MediaPunch /IPX, p. 6; AP Photo/Rebecca Blackwell, p. 7; AP Photo/The Yomiuri Shimbun, p. 8; William STEVENS/Gamma-Rapho/Getty Images, p. 9; Koji Watanabe/Getty Images, pp. 10, 16; Ezra Shaw/Getty Images, pp. 12, 13; KAZUHIRO NOGI/AFP/Getty Images, p. 15; Power Sport Images/Getty Images, p. 17; Al Bello/Getty Images, p. 18; Kyodo News Stills/Getty Images, p. 19; AP Photo/Seth Wenig, p. 21; AP Photo/Jason Heidrich/Icon Sportswire, p. 22; Tim Clayton/Corbis/Getty Images, p. 23; AP Photo/Press Association, p. 25; Mark Metcalfe/Getty Images, p. 26; AP Photo/Hussein Sayed, p. 27.

Cover: AP Photo/John Cordes/Icon Sportswire.